£10.99
746.92

Vivienne Westwood

SEAN CONNOLLY

Heinemann
LIBRARY

www.heinemann.co.uk/library
Visit our website to find out more information about **Heinemann Library** books.

To order:
☎ Phone 44 (0) 1865 888066
🗎 Send a fax to 44 (0) 1865 314091
🖳 Visit the Heinemann Bookshop at www.heinemann.co.uk/library to browse our catalogue and order online.

First published in Great Britain by Heinemann Library, Halley Court, Jordan Hill, Oxford OX2 8EJ, a division of Reed Educational and Professional Publishing Ltd. Heinemann is a registered trademark of Reed Educational and Professional Publishing Ltd.

OXFORD MELBOURNE AUCKLAND JOHANNESBURG BLANTYRE
GABORONE IBADAN PORTSMOUTH NH (USA) CHICAGO

© Reed Educational and Professional Publishing Ltd 2002
The moral right of the proprietor has been asserted.

Designed by Tinstar Design (www.tinstar.co.uk)
Originated by Ambassador Litho Ltd
Printed and bound by South China Printing Company Ltd in Hong Kong/China

ISBN 0 431 13999 7
06 05 04 03 02
10 9 8 7 6 5 4 3 2 1

British Library Cataloguing in Publication Data
Connolly, Sean
      Vivienne Westwood. – (Creative Lives)
      1. Westwood, Vivienne
      2. Women designers – England – Biography – Juvenile literature
      3. Sculptors – England – Biography – Juvenile literature
      I.Title
      730.9'2

Acknowledgements
The Publishers would like to thank the following for permission to reproduce photographs: Aerofilm: p38; Corbis: Laszio Veres p6, Bettmann p14, Denis O'Regan p36, Dave Bartruff p43; Francis Frith Collection: pp10, 15; Hulton Archive: pp23, 33; Museum of London: pp49, 51; Press Association: p48; Pymca: Ted Polhemus p39; Redferns: Dave Ellis p25, Ian Dickson p28, Virginia Turbett p30; Rex Features: pp26, 40, 50, 54, Nils Jorgensen p19, Today p47; Topham Picturepoint: pp4, 5, 8, 20, 21, 22, 24, 31; University of Westminster Archive: p16; Victoria & Albert Museum: p35, 53, Daniel McGrath p29; Virgin Records: p32; Vivienne Westwood Press Office: pp12, 27, 42, 45, 52.

Cover photograph reproduced with permission of Retna.

Picture research by Kay Altwegg.

Our thanks to Murray Blewitt and the Vivienne Westwood Press Office for their assistance in the preparation of this book.

Every effort has been made to contact copyright holders of any material reproduced in this book. Any omissions will be rectified in subsequent printings if notice is given to the Publisher.

Disclaimer
All the Internet addresses (URLs) given in this book were valid at the time of going to press. However, due to the dynamic nature of the Internet, some addresses may have changed, or sites may have changed or ceased to exist since publication. While the author and Publishers regret any inconvenience this may cause readers, no responsibility for any such changes can be accepted by either the author or the Publishers.

Contents

Any words appearing in the text in bold, **like this**, are explained in the Glossary.

The contrary trendsetter

Very few people in Britain have managed – or dared – to suggest overthrowing the Royal Family and then made the trip to Buckingham Palace to receive an honour from the Queen. The designer Vivienne Westwood did exactly that, in the space of just over a decade. And she felt no contradiction in judging Britain from both sides of the Palace gates. What sort of person can change from an **anarchist** to a treasured member of the British **Establishment**? And what might account for such a dramatic change of heart? Or even more to the point, has there even been a change of heart?

Vivienne Westwood has managed this delicate balancing act. She is one of a handful of international designers whose names are familiar to ordinary people around the world. Her clothes sell, and are admired greatly, in many countries. Yet it is her home country, the United Kingdom, which is central to her life. Whether celebrating the clothes of some of Britain's 'tribes', or deliberately shocking the **conservative** British Establishment, Vivienne Westwood has always been linked with Britain.

Vivienne Westwood has never been afraid to model her own creations. Here she is attending a fashion tribute in her honour at the Victoria & Albert Museum in London in 1998.

Turning tradition on its head

The world of fashion has traditionally been surrounded by an atmosphere of wealth and **decorum**. Leading designers, employing dozens of assistants and business advisers, produce one range of clothes (known as a collection) every six months. They show these clothes in one of the leading fashion cities – Paris in France, Milan in Italy or London. Showing these ranges is important and the designers work hard to create and maintain a specific style that fashion writers and

Vivienne Westwood confounded her critics – and many of her supporters – when she was awarded the OBE in 1992.

buyers will recognize immediately. With so much at stake – staff salaries, office rentals, advertising, the cost of the shows themselves – designers cannot afford to make huge changes to this 'look'. Ambitious young designers usually need to start at the bottom in big firms, and then work their way up, much as people do in other large companies. Vivienne Westwood turned that career path on its head.

With her poor background, she was denied a chance to buy the **haute couture** clothes she saw in the pages of fashion magazines as a young woman. This background, however, worked to her advantage. She was able to produce her designs – oozing with what would now be called **street credibility** – because she herself was a member of the groups she clothed.

5

Finding a voice

Many of the groups that Westwood clothed stood outside the mainstream of British society as rebels. Along with her former partner Malcolm McLaren, Vivienne lived the life of the rock-and-roll loving **Teddy Boys**. Later, she turned to the provocative outfits that inspired the **Punks**. When other better-known designers caught up with her, producing 'safer' versions of her designs, Vivienne turned to yet more groups for inspiration: pirates for example. Along the way, and despite her growing reputation, Vivienne Westwood maintained her links with her early designing days in the 1970s. She even refused to move from her cluttered flat in south London, which she and McLaren lived in when they were struggling to make ends meet.

Despite being denied the social privileges that would have given her an easier route to a successful career as a designer, Vivienne Westwood has made the best of some natural advantages. Of course, she possesses natural talent, but she was also influenced by her independent-minded mother, who gave her a sound background in sewing and clothes-making generally. And Vivienne's interest in fashion throughout history has enabled her to examine historical designs – from classical Greece, 16th-century Germany or Revolutionary France – to determine precisely why each stitch or seam goes in a particular place. By understanding the historical source of her inspiration, Westwood has been able to build on old designs and give them a new spirit.

The best of British

Vivienne Westwood is as well known in New York or Tokyo as she is in London. But it is her deep understanding of British society – its unique balance of conservatism and daring design – that is at the root of her creations. It seems that no element of British society has escaped her notice. And it is not just the human element of British life that figures so highly. Vivienne Westwood also appreciates, as few others do, the potential of British materials such as tweeds and woollens. 'I'm a rebel but not an outsider' seems a good motto for someone who has created outfits made solely of carpet material, and invented her own Scottish clan in order to register a tartan of her own design!

7

A northern childhood

The hills, towns and cities of the area around Manchester and Sheffield illustrate many people's idea of the typical industrial landscape of northern England. The hills are carpeted in wild flowers and tall grass in the spring, but are dark and brooding through the long, rainy winter. Scattered throughout this dramatic scenery are villages and towns which, in the 1800s, developed into important centres for producing textiles. Today, labourers' cottages still line the streets alongside brick-built mills and factories.

It is this 'typically' northern landscape – part industrial and part rural – that Vivienne Westwood calls home. She was born Vivienne Isabel Swire on 8 April 1941, in the Derbyshire village of Tintwistle. Her parents, Gordon and Dora, were local people who had married two years earlier.

Shaped by the war

The war brought many dangers and hardships to the British people. Manchester, just ten miles from Tintwistle, was badly bombed. The Swires and other villagers would have seen the bright glow of burning buildings against the night sky. Young men from the village were away with the armed services, causing more concern for the small community.

In other respects, the war brought stability and even a little prosperity to the Swires. Gordon, who had worked at his parents' grocery shop before the war, found work in a factory producing aircraft near Manchester. Dora worked as a weaver in a local cotton factory, helping to produce equipment such as parachutes, tents, balloons and uniforms for the war effort. The Swires even managed to have a family car, which represented a luxury in their village during the war years.

The family also began to grow. A second child, Olga, was born in early 1944 and a third, Gordon, followed two years later. Born either during the war, or immediately after it, the three children developed in a society that valued being careful with money. The British economy had been badly shaken by the war, and it took many years to recover. The Labour government, led by Clement Attlee, which was elected soon after the war ended, tried to keep up the 'British spirit' and willingness to make sacrifices that had helped the nation through the dark years of the war. 'Make do and mend' – as opposed to buying something new – was a typical **slogan**. And Dora Swire, with her sewing skills, was well placed to do just that.

Free spirit at work

Vivienne's parents did not push their children into studying hard at school. In fact, they rarely even looked at their school reports. They

This view of Tintwistle shows the village in the 1960s, much as it looked during Vivienne Westwood's childhood.

Early rebellion

Cotton remained the most important industry in the area, employing up to 80 per cent of the local workforce in the early 20th century. Dora Swire worked in the mills, and was able to put her skills and experience to good use at home. Using off-cuts and remnants of material from the factory, she was able to make clothes for her family and even dresses for her own passion – ballroom dancing.

Vivienne inherited her mother's ability and sense of flair with clothing. In her early teens, she would come home from school with a bit of material and transform it into a dress that same evening. She also used her skills to daring effect by 'customizing' her conservative grammar school uniform. Seeking to create a sexy appearance, Vivienne tightened the skirt around her hips and added a slit up the back.

did, however, encourage Vivienne, Olga and Gordon to develop a love for the countryside that surrounded them. The three children spent many happy hours collecting wild flowers, making 'lemonade' from fresh blossoms and berries, and rambling across the hills and valleys near their home.

Such playing appealed to Vivienne's sense of creativity. Leading her brother and sister on rambles – as well as knowing that her parents did not expect strict obedience in school – also made Vivienne extremely independent. On her first day of nursery school, she had what she later described jokingly as her 'first confrontation with **tyranny**'. Noticing a long queue outside the girls' lavatory, she decided that rules were there to be broken and simply used the boys' lavatory instead!

Confrontations with authority continued through Vivienne's early school years, but she did well enough academically to go on to Glossop Grammar School, about three miles from her home.

A new London home

By the early 1950s, competition from other countries was affecting the British textile industry and jobs became scarcer in areas that depended on textile mills for employment. Gordon had a job in a local ice-cream factory, but had to supplement his income by doing odd jobs for neighbours.

Vivienne aged sixteen. It was at this time that the Swires moved to Harrow in London, taking Vivienne with them.

In 1954, Dora Swire became village postmistress in Tintwistle. The new position, which provided both housing and a steady income, was well timed. It was also significant that the post office business was in Dora's name, setting an example of female independence to Vivienne.

Vivienne continued to study at Glossop Grammar School, making her mark as a popular but argumentative girl. She sought attention by wearing daring outfits such as high-heeled shoes, slinky dresses and large outrageous earrings. Fashion magazines and Hollywood films provided her with examples and inspiration. She and her best friend Maureen Purcell would make trips to Manchester and Leeds to check on new fashions. Maureen had relatives in the tailoring business in both of these cities.

The move to London

By 1957, Gordon was unemployed, and the income from the Tintwistle post office was not enough to support the family. Late in that year, though, Vivienne's parents were offered a similar post office position in Harrow, a residential district in northwest London. The family decided to make the move south.

Vivienne must have been excited to be living so close to the heart of Britain's social life. London fashion shows, its Hollywood film premieres at West End cinemas and the **pageantry** of the Royal Family (Queen Elizabeth's Coronation had taken place just four years before) seemed to lie on her doorstep. The reality proved to be far less exciting. Harrow, although only several miles from the bright lights and bustle of the West End, was very different in social terms. Its mainly working-class population spent their lives within a small area, separated from the glamorous West End by education, money and social standing.

Nevertheless the Swires made a go of their Harrow post office and grocery store, selling children's clothes in the front and making enough money for Gordon to take on another shop in nearby Stanmore. Vivienne briefly attended Harrow Art School, but abandoned her course in silversmithing and jewellery-making to train as a teacher.

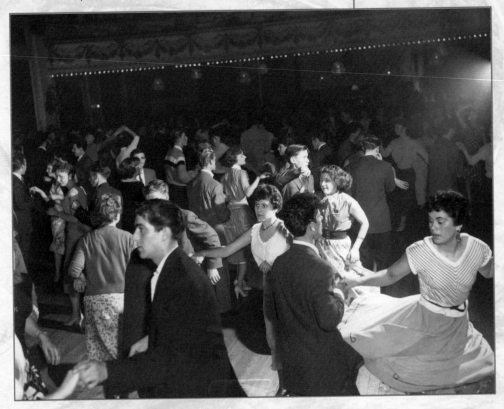

London teenagers dance to rock and roll music in September 1959. It was at a dance like this that Vivienne met Derek Westwood, who was soon to become her first husband.

New beginnings

Vivienne got a job teaching at a primary school in Willesden, near Harrow. Her main source of entertainment was dancing, although Vivienne preferred the new-style rock and roll to the ballroom dancing that her parents loved so much. It was at a dance in 1961 that Vivienne met Derek John Westwood who, at 23, was only two years older than Vivienne. Derek proposed marriage, Vivienne accepted, and they married in July 1962. Just over a year later their son, Benjamin Arthur Westwood, was born. The family ended up living less than a quarter of a mile from the Swires' Harrow post office.

Full-time teaching was out of the question, so Vivienne took a part-time job cutting rolls of film at the local Kodak factory. At only 22 years of age, she was married, with a small child and a boring job, and living just a stone's throw from her parents. The days of teenage rebellion and daring fashion statements now seemed behind her.

Birth of the teenager

The mid-1950s, at about the time that Vivienne's family moved to London, saw a profound social change – the rise of the teenager. There was no more **rationing** of goods and unemployment was low, meaning that families had more money to spend. Also ready to spend their money was a new generation: teenagers who had been born during or shortly after the war. Like teenagers in America (and sometimes following their example in fashion and music), Britain's teenagers were eager to enjoy themselves and to rebel against what was left of the old **conservatism**. They spent money at record shops and coffee bars, and many found another way to express their rebellion – with colourful and outrageous clothes.

Station Road, Harrow, defined the edge of Vivienne's world in the early 1960s.

Metropolitan milestones

Derek Westwood had been an apprentice in a local factory when he met Vivienne, but he had ambitions to break free of his working-class background by becoming an airline pilot. By the time the two were married, he had got a job in the airline industry, as a steward for British European Airways. But despite Derek's optimism, Vivienne still felt rooted to a conventional, dreary way of life. It was through her younger brother Gordon that she managed to find a way out.

Students queue to enrol at Harrow Art School. It was here that Malcolm McLaren and Gordon Swire, Vivienne's brother, were to meet in the 1960s.

Student life

Gordon, like Vivienne, had enrolled at the Harrow Art School, but unlike Vivienne, he had carried on with his studies in theatre design and built up a circle of friends there. These young people, still in their teens, stayed up late, drinking coffee and cheap wine, discussing art and how Britain's political and social landscape could only be changed through **revolution**. They had a completely different outlook on life from the more conventional people that Vivienne was used to.

One of the most interesting of these students was a young man named Malcolm McLaren (who at that time went by his stepfather's surname of Edwards). McLaren, like others in Gordon's circle, was rebellious and cynical. He also had a way of drawing attention to himself through his clothing. At this point in the mid-1960s, he had adopted the style of the **Mods**, who favoured tight-fitting jackets worn over neat white shirts, slim trousers and desert boots – a reaction to the baggy, traditional male outfits of the 1940s and 1950s.

McLaren's appearance and attitude appealed to Vivienne. She began to spend more time back at the Swire family home, where Gordon would feed Malcolm once Dora was busy at the post office counter. Dora did not approve of this young friend, who slept in Gordon's old car parked outside the house. Vivienne, on the other hand, was intrigued by McLaren's energy, sarcastic wit and desire for attention. She spent more and more time with Gordon and Malcolm, drifting further from her husband.

Malcolm offered her a glimpse into a different, more exciting world. 'I felt there were so many doors to open, and he had the key to all of them,' she recalled some years later.

At the same time, though, Vivienne acted as a positive influence on Malcolm. McLaren had been brought up by an eccentric grandmother who had spoiled him at times and enforced her will strongly at others. With Vivienne, he began to develop a relationship that was based on mutual respect and affection.

A new relationship

By 1966, Derek and Vivienne had grown completely apart and they divorced. At about the same time, Vivienne and Malcolm began a new relationship. After living briefly with Gordon when he got a flat of his own, the couple found their own flat in south London. Malcolm had enrolled at the nearby Croydon College of Art and Design. By this time, Vivienne was pregnant again. Her second son, christened Joseph Ferdinand, was born on 30 November 1967. Joseph's surname of Corré, chosen by his parents, was that of Malcolm's grandmother.

Malcolm had a hard time coming to terms with fatherhood, believing it to restrict his ambition and personal freedom. Vivienne, however, saw things differently. She believed that their child provided a bond for the couple's relationship. Despite her happiness at Joseph's birth, she found herself forced to return to work as a teacher only six weeks later.

Art school politics

The inspiration behind the image of 'Swinging London' during the 1960s came in large part from the graduates of Britain's art schools and colleges. These schools encouraged artistic freedom and a willingness to blur the boundaries between different types of art – and between art and life.

Malcolm McLaren was very much part of this 'art school scene'. By the time he and Vivienne were living together, he had become influenced by the Situationists, a group of **radical** European thinkers. The Situationists believed that artists needed to break down the boundaries between art and life. By creating absurd (and even shocking) 'situations', they felt they would upset and eventually destroy old-fashioned society. This combination of radical politics, artistic ambition and **absurdist** practical jokes appealed greatly to Malcolm. It would also later provide a source of inspiration for Vivienne as she gained fame as a designer.

Money was tight, but Vivienne was willing to make sacrifices for her unpredictable relationship with Malcolm. It was a way of life that would continue for many years.

Style warrior

Malcolm McLaren offered the perfect way out of conventional and predictable married life for Vivienne. 'I was excited by this idea of taking culture to the streets and changing the whole way of life, using culture as a means of making trouble,' he once said. 'Making trouble' could take all sorts of forms. At one point he was part of a group that barricaded itself inside the Croydon College of Art and Design, demanding to be allowed to sculpt in pure gold. On another occasion, he and a group of others began giving away toys from Selfridges department store in central London.

However, real change seemed to be occurring in Paris, France. The year 1968 saw French students, immigrants, workers and trade unionists combining in a series of strikes that threatened to overthrow the French government. McLaren joined the thousands of young foreigners in what the French later called *les évenements* ('the events') of May 1968.

May 1968 saw many battles between students and riot police in Paris, France. Malcolm McLaren was one of thousands of young foreigners who lent their support to the striking students.

Vivienne, meanwhile, was back in London working and looking after her two young sons. Malcolm's letters from France described the scenes in Paris and also Marseille, and invited Vivienne to join him. Leaving her sons with her mother, she travelled to meet Malcolm. They spent several weeks together, living in a tent. Apart from a brief school trip to Switzerland, it was her first experience of a foreign country.

Vivienne and Malcolm were a devoted – if somewhat unconventional – couple in the 1960s.

More changes

Returning to London, Vivienne found that Joseph had reacted badly to her absence. She therefore felt even more need to provide comfort and support for her children. At the same time, Malcolm was feeling more tied down by the same family commitments. He went off on his own again, leaving Vivienne and the boys to cope alone. Vivienne left her teaching job and settled briefly with her parents (who had by then retired to Oxfordshire) before then moving to live in her aunt's caravan in North Wales.

She supported herself and the boys on the small amount of money she received from the government. Recalling her own long nature walks as a child, she took them on rambles in the Welsh countryside. The boys flourished. However, Malcolm had now found a flat in Clapham (South London) and in 1970 the four of them moved into this new home. Then, reacting to the lack of discipline she had seen as a teacher, Vivienne decided to send both boys to boarding school. She was alone with Malcolm for the first time, apart from their brief trip to France.

21

Hippy life

The most powerful youth movement of the late 1960s and early 1970s was that of the hippies. Originating in San Francisco, California in the mid-1960s, the hippies typified what we now see as 'Sixties values' – peace, drugs and **free love**. At first their outfits were a deliberate effort to oppose conservative styles: long-haired men and women wore flowers, criticized violence and hoped to create a society that would be built on trust and mutual respect. By the late 1960s, these aims seemed impossible to achieve and many people adopted the lifestyle simply to drop out of society. Moreover, by around 1970, it had become obvious to Malcolm and Vivienne that the hippy lifestyle was starting to revolve merely around fashion and music, rather than people's desire to change society.

Although at first the hippies of the late 1960s hoped to change the world, by the early 1970s the hippy lifestyle had become little more than a fashion statement.

Let it Rock

By now Vivienne was almost 30 years old, but in many respects she was just finding herself as an individual. She decided to join McLaren in his open defiance of the popular **hippy** fashion. Their weapon – as it would be in the future – was clothing. The pair of them chose the fashion of the **Teddy Boys**, a group whose clothing style and taste in music was linked to the 1950s rather than the 1960s or 1970s. Vivienne and Malcolm would parade themselves, in Teddy Boy-style unconventional clothes, along the King's Road, the capital of London's fashion trendsetters, exhibiting (in Malcolm's words) 'the beauty of fearlessness'.

Malcolm's art school days finally ended in 1971, and he had to think of a way of earning money. Whilst in London one day, he was offered the chance to set up a small shop (selling rock and roll souvenirs and clothing) at 430 King's Road. The address was at the unfashionable, and less expensive, end of this famous London fashion 'centre'. Let it Rock, the name chosen by Malcolm and Vivienne for their new venture, opened in November 1971.

A Teddy Boy pictured in the mid-1950s. Vivienne and Malcolm copied the Teddy-Boy look for their new range of clothing to be sold at the Let it Rock shop.

23

Truth going naked

Vivienne and Malcolm now had a base for their assault on popular fashion. The Let it Rock shop sold all sorts of items relating to the 'golden age' of rock and roll: the 1950s. The pair scoured London's markets for records, posters, magazines and even bits of furniture. But the real attraction for them was the clothing – jackets, thin ties and narrow **drainpipe** trousers for men, and full 'hoop' skirts, cardigans, white bobby socks and lace-up shoes for women.

Entering the shop was like walking back in time. The old jukebox played classic rock and roll songs, by Elvis Presley, Eddy Cochrane and Little Richard. At first business was slow, then Vivienne and Malcolm started to visit some of the **Teddy Boy** haunts in London's East End, handing out cards with details of the shop. This 'word-of-mouth'

advertising helped Let it Rock build a reputation; the relaxed atmosphere of the shop helped it grow into a social centre of its own. Then other members of the public – either the curious, or those who enjoyed what would now be described as the **retro** feel – began to buy.

Vivienne's experience as a dressmaker began to come into its own. At first she limited herself to carrying out repairs to the worn or frayed second-hand clothing she was selling,

Vivienne had become immersed in the business of repairing and designing clothes by the time Let it Rock made a name for itself.

Patterns for the future

Vivienne's work at Let it Rock sowed the seeds for her subsequent career. With the occasional help of an experienced London tailor named Sid Green, she painstakingly re-created a whole range of rock and roll outfits. She would use an original garment and then take it apart seam by seam, noticing exactly how each element related to other parts of the garment. Then she would use **authentic** buttons, linings and other features to complete the work. She would also sometimes use fake fur, brightly coloured cloth or more unusual materials to add a note of independent creativity. At the heart of Vivienne's work lay her desire to investigate the originals that inspired her own work.

American band the New York Dolls were regular customers of Vivienne and Malcolm.

The 'dangerous' look of the biker's leathers was a real attraction for Vivienne and Malcolm's second shop, Too Fast to Live Too Young to Die. Vivienne was beginning to push the boundaries of what constituted 'good taste'.

generally doing whatever was needed to make the goods saleable. She and Malcolm were only able to afford her second-hand sewing machine by having the telephone disconnected at their flat. But simple repairs proved to be not enough as demand for Let it Rock outfits outstripped supply. It was time to create clothes from scratch.

Pushing the limits

Let it Rock had become something of a landmark, attracting rock stars, film directors and journalists as customers. Malcolm was constantly at the shop, while Vivienne usually worked behind the scenes. By the end of 1972, however, the pair began to tire of the Teddy Boy clothes they were selling. Vivienne in particular also felt that the Teddy Boy image had racist and sexist overtones. It was time for a change. So, Let it Rock reopened under a new name – Too Fast to Live Too Young to Die (TFTLTYTD) – in 1973.

The new shop's image was also rebellious, featuring the clothing and styles of another rebel group: the **bikers**. Menacing black, studded leather jackets, chains and other motorcycle related items replaced the rock and roll clothing of Let it Rock. Vivienne and Malcolm also took another element of the biker's wardrobe – the white T-shirt – and began to give it their own touches.

With her characteristic attention to detail, Vivienne printed and stencilled **slogans** on to the T-shirts. On others she sewed pieces of letter-shaped bones to create menacing messages. To Vivienne, these clothes were statements that would shake society out of its **conservatism**. Her own look, complete with spiked hair and skull earrings, was in tune with the goods she was creating and selling. It was also attention-grabbing: *West One* magazine featured her as one of 'London's Belles' in its December 1973 issue.

The shop front of SEX, Vivienne and Malcolm's third shop at 430 King's Road, London.

Malcolm, pleased with the success of TFTLTYTD, nevertheless wanted to create more **controversy**. Fascinated by the **provocative** image of the stars Lou Reed, Iggy Pop and David Bowie, he decided that sex was a subject that was sure to stir up the emotions of the British. With that in mind, he and Vivienne closed TFTLTYTD in April 1974, after just over a year in business. About four months later, the shop at 430 King's Road reopened under a new name: SEX. Customers entered through a doorway spray-painted with a quote from the French philosopher Jean-Jacques Rousseau: 'Craft must have clothes but Truth loves to go naked.'

Clothing the Punks

SEX was the third of Vivienne and Malcolm's shops at the same address. The previous versions had either catered to an existing market (such as those looking for **authentic** rock and roll outfits) or had created demand for items that the public had never before valued highly. This time, though, Vivienne and Malcolm would be masterminding a fashion movement that would sweep across Britain and around the world.

The working arrangements also pointed the way to the future, and gave a sign of how Vivienne and Malcolm would ultimately drift apart. Malcolm still had his eyes on the music world, and he seemed determined to take an active role in that area, ideally as a band manager. To Vivienne, however, the new shop was an opportunity to develop her ideas about shocking society through fashion. The whole atmosphere of SEX was designed to shock, with sex toys and **pornographic** cartoons on display in the shop.

Vivienne was also building on the dressmaking techniques that she had used since childhood. T-shirts were one example. Most people agreed that nothing could be more basic than a T-shirt. Vivienne disagreed and

Vivienne during the Punk era, pictured with Sid Vicious of the Sex Pistols.

decided to take the garment's design a stage further. Using the same technique that she had used with **Teddy Boy** outfits from the 1950s, she took T-shirts apart seam by seam, deciding what was necessary and what was **superfluous**. Sleeves, she decided, were 'extras', and she therefore designed T-shirts that were just two rectangles of fabric sewn together.

From there, it was a small step to other details that would later become linked with the **Punk** movement, such as sexually aggressive **slogans** and tears in clothes exposing flesh. Working mainly from her own cramped flat, Vivienne would print T-shirts and alter by hand rubber clothing that she ordered in bulk from sex catalogues. Although the term 'Punk' was not yet widely used, she was developing a way of producing clothes that would be **synonymous** with punk fashion – Do-It-Yourself.

The Punk 'outfit' has become one of the most recognizable images of the 1970s.

The classic punk outfit
Vivienne combined many influences to inspire the Punk 'look' that so many young people (and later, mainstream fashion designers) would copy. The most typical outfit comprised **bondage** trousers (strapped together at the knees), mohair (a type of wool) sweater and a T-shirt with a slogan on it, and echoed the clothing on sale at SEX. The overall effect was to shock and overturn notions of what constituted good taste.

The Sex Pistols, with their provocative lead singer Johnny Rotten, were ideal models for Vivienne's challenging new designs.

The Sex Pistols

SEX attracted a loyal following of customers as well as part-time staff, all inspired by the outrageous image of the shop and its clothes. Among their regular customers was a pair of teenagers from West London, Paul Cook and Steve Jones. Together they made up a band called Kutie Jones, and a friend played one of their tapes to McLaren. Malcolm decided to take them under his wing so that he could break into the music business himself. He found a vocalist, John Lydon, to front the band. Renamed Johnny Rotten, Lydon was the last piece of the McLaren jigsaw puzzle. The band, now called the Sex Pistols, was launched in the autumn of 1975.

McLaren wanted the band to promote the shop and vice versa. Vivienne and some of the shop assistants set about creating a 'look' for the Sex Pistols. The band members, who were pleased that their outfits would be provided free of charge, had some say in the process. Johnny Rotten, for example, was the first to use safety pins as a fashion accessory.

'Nothing more important in culture has happened since. I think it is important that kids have an understanding of that movement. That they [the Sex Pistols] were not just another pop act.'
Film-maker Julien Temple, quoted in the Toronto *Globe and Mail*, 27 January 2000

The first Sex Pistols concert was on 6 November 1975 at St Martin's College of Art in central London. The concert was hardly a success in musical terms, but the band soon had a devoted following, whose outfits echoed the 'Do-It-Yourself' nature of Vivienne's clothes at SEX. These young people, the first real Punks, helped the Sex Pistols – and in turn, SEX – gain even more publicity. The band had few musical skills, but the outrageous fans, the threatening song lyrics and the band's apparent association with sex and violence created a **critical momentum**.

Punks in the 1970s. The shocking and outrageous clothing worn by Punk bands and their fans made Vivienne and Malcolm's shop SEX more popular than ever.

God Save the Queen

In October 1976, McLaren got a record deal for the Sex Pistols. Their first single, 'Anarchy in the UK', was released soon afterwards. The boundaries between music and fashion, business and **propaganda** were blurred, as both Vivienne and Malcolm helped to write the words to the **inflammatory** song, which became a huge hit. And in keeping with the song's message about rebellion and **sedition**, Vivienne and Malcolm once again changed the name of their shop, this time to Seditionaries. The new shop sign celebrated 'Clothes for Heroes'.

With Malcolm acting as something of an **impresario**, the Punk movement gained more and more publicity. 'Punks love to be hated',

The cover of the widely banned Sex Pistols single 'God Save the Queen', designed by Jamie Reed, used some of the same 'cut-and-paste' techniques as Vivienne's clothing designs.

Vivienne appearing outside court after the Jubilee boat incident in 1977.

boasted one young fan. The Sex Pistols, encouraged by Malcolm, did their best to help this process. In 1977, the year of Queen Elizabeth's **Silver Jubilee**, they released 'God Save the Queen', a fierce criticism of British society. The song reached number one in the charts, although many record shops refused to stock it. To celebrate the Jubilee itself, the band performed on a specially hired boat on the River Thames. As the party grew more uncontrollable, fighting broke out and the River Police ordered the boat back to shore. Amid all the confusion, both Vivienne and Malcolm were arrested. Although Richard Branson (for whose Virgin record label the Sex Pistols were by then recording) got them out of jail the next day, the pair believed they had made their mark.

Not by accident but design

The **Silver Jubilee** Year (1977), complete with the arrests of Vivienne and Malcolm, marked the high point of the **Punk** era. The Sex Pistols, despite arrests, broadcast bans and a number of personal problems (including rumours that band member Sid Vicious was becoming heavily involved with drugs), had become extremely popular and famous. The Punk movement spread far beyond Britain. While things were at their peak, Vivienne and Malcolm grew famous for their contributions to Punk: Malcolm for the music and the sense of theatre he brought to the Sex Pistols' careers, and Vivienne for the eye-catching designs that put her at the forefront of the fashion **avant garde**.

But the creative and romantic partnership of Vivienne and Malcolm was nearly over. He had been spending very little time at the shop, concentrating on music and also forming relationships with other women. When the Sex Pistols finally split up in 1978, he went to Paris for a year. Back in London, Vivienne, who had put so much of her spirit into Punk fashion, saw her designs being copied and made 'safe' by commercial designers. Safety pins and mock cigarette holes in dresses were cropping up in high street shops. Just as the whole **Teddy Boy** scene had begun to seem stale in the early 1970s, now Punk seemed to be running out of steam – at least in Vivienne's eyes.

Turning to museums

Vivienne had gained confidence as a designer through her association with Punk. The outfits worn by Punks, as well as those on the rails at the Seditionaries shop, seemed shocking and outrageous, but they reflected the research and great care that Vivienne applied to all her work. Now she wanted to put these qualities to work in a different direction. She began spending a great deal of time in London's museums and galleries. Although she had no formal art training, her interest in art (and design) history had been developed through her contact with Malcolm and his art college friends.

She was particularly interested in the Wallace Collection museum and the costume collection of the Victoria & Albert Museum, and in the fashion of the eighteenth century. With her keen eye and attention to detail, she noticed that the designers of that period had a drastically different approach to fashion. Instead of designing clothes that would follow the lines of the body, they deliberately created folds and sags that moved while the person walked. This discovery also appealed to Vivienne's contrary streak. New Wave, the musical and fashion movement that came after Punk, prized **minimalist**, tight clothing. Vivienne, on the other hand, decided to create clothes that were flowing and billowing.

An example of the 18th-century clothing in the Victoria & Albert Museum, which Vivienne found so inspiring.

Urban pirates

It was at about this time that Malcolm returned from Paris. Although the relationship between the couple seemed to be less intense, he still had the power to influence Vivienne's design ideas. Malcolm had noticed a new trend emerging in London's clubs – that of the New Romantics. These young people, with their long hair and vivid make-up, preferred lavish outfits that seemed rooted in the age of swordfights and duels. In other words, they seemed to be on the same wavelength as Vivienne. Examining Vivienne's designs, Malcolm concluded that the ordinary young person would not be interested in the eighteenth century. He suggested adapting the design ideas to celebrate the pirate look, since pirates – like Punks and the Teddy Boys of the 1950s – were rebels, and rebellion was always popular.

Vivienne tinkers with the 'Pirate' look of Annabella, lead singer of Bow Wow Wow.

Malcolm also had a new band, Bow Wow Wow, to promote. He planned to re-create the success of combining music and clothing by dressing the band members in the new 'pirate' outfits. Seditionaries was closed and boarded up to create mystery and anticipation. It reopened in 1980 as World's End, its interior resembling the decking of a pirate ship. The shop, and the outfits, attracted enormous publicity. Bow Wow Wow, however, failed to have anything like the impact that the Sex Pistols had. This was not a huge concern for Vivienne because she had something else in mind: taking on the fashion world head-on.

To do that, and to gain real recognition from the industry's powerful fashion journalists, she decided to show her 'Pirates' collection formally as a collection in March 1981. Most designers build their whole careers around these twice-yearly **catwalk** displays, preparing for the next collection almost as soon as the first has taken place. For Vivienne it was very different. There was a frantic rush as she assembled the clothes, mainly in her own cramped flat. With some help from her loyal shop assistants, she was ironing billowing Pirate shirts, stitching seams and hand-pleating silk right up to the night before her show.

Fashion collections

The fashion industry operates according to a rigid system of shows, called 'collections', which Vivienne entered with 'Pirates' in March 1981. Leading designers display their latest **lines** every six months, featuring clothes that can be worn six months later. Members of the fashion press as well as buyers for the major high-fashion clothing outlets around the world attend these shows. A well-received collection is a huge boost for a designer, leading to many orders and large profits. The first Westwood collection succeeded almost in spite of the fact that Vivienne had either ignored or disregarded some of the traditions. Unlike most designers, she had decorated the hall with Pirate **motifs**, in keeping with the theme of the clothes. And unlike most designers, who remain backstage during the show, Vivienne was out front and enjoying the spectacle.

The show created a buzz of anticipation around London and there were even fights to get tickets. The show was held in one of the halls in the Olympia Exhibition Centre in West London. Even as the Bow Wow Wow accompanying music was beginning, Vivienne and a team of assistants were putting the finishing touches to the clothes. The show itself was an exciting affair, totally in keeping with the theme of the clothes. Models appeared in a fog of dry ice and walked down the catwalk to the sound of cannon fire.

The response was just as electrifying. The audience, which included pop stars such as Mick Jagger and Boy George, was thrilled. Just as importantly, members of the 'serious' fashion press applauded the collection. *Women's Wear Daily*, one of the most influential fashion magazines, wrote 'Westwood is the hottest designer of the new look'. And **buyers** were equally impressed. The biggest boost, from Vivienne's point of view, came when the **curator** of 20th-century dress at the Victoria & Albert Museum asked for a **custom-made** outfit for the permanent collection. At that point, Vivienne knew that she had made her mark.

London's prestigious Olympia Exhibition Centre, where Vivienne's 'Pirates' collection was first shown in March 1981.

A model poses outside the World's End shop in an outfit from Westwood's 'Pirates' collection.

Back to her roots

Fashion magazines such as *Vanity Fair* and *Vogue* featured Vivienne's 'Pirates' collection. *The Sunday Times* reported that the pirate look was catching on with the 'smart set' of Chelsea and Kensington – far removed from the people who used to buy Vivienne's clothes.

Vivienne and Malcolm McLaren in October 1981. Despite appearances, their relationship was coming to a close.

" *'She didn't want to be part of this rock 'n' roll mentality any more, and all my stuff was about music.'* **"**

Malcolm McLaren, recognizing his own lessened influence on Vivienne in the early 1980s

For Vivienne, it was also a time of great personal change. Malcolm moved out of the flat shortly after the 'Pirates' show, bringing their relationship to a close. The pair would, however, remain linked on a professional level for another five years. No longer linked romantically with Malcolm, Vivienne severed her ties with the music world.

Freed from a connection that had become stifling and limiting, Vivienne was able to explore areas of fashion and learning that Malcolm had scorned. In one sense, Vivienne was discovering the value of 'tradition', but in another it was a way for her to widen the sources of her inspiration. She just needed a little guidance.

Influential acquaintances

In the early 1980s, Vivienne became friendly with two men who would become influential supports in the coming years. The first was a Canadian artist named Gary Ness. Having trained as an artist in Paris, Ness became a portrait painter, briefly, in America before settling in England. He and Vivienne hit it off immediately, with Ness assuming the role of her cultural **mentor** in art and literature. The pair would talk for hours about the relative merits of different artists and paintings, novelists and poets, and **aesthetics** generally.

The second person was an Italian named Carlo D'Amario, whom Vivienne met in Paris. With a varied background that included dealing in Arabian rugs and even pinball machines, D'Amario was experienced in business. Like Ness, he drew Vivienne away from the memory of McLaren's influence by pointing out how influential (and wealthy) she could become by concentrating on the fashion industry. An on-again, off-again personal relationship also developed between the two, but D'Amario's lasting influence has been to keep the Westwood fashion line successful in commercial terms.

Triumph and trauma

A second collection, called 'Savage', was shown in London in October 1981. The bold and colourful designs were based on Vivienne's research on tribes in developing countries. Vivienne and Malcolm opened a second shop, called Nostalgia of Mud, in central London. They also decided that the next collection, 'Buffalo' (October 1982), would be shown in the heart of the fashion world – Paris. The last British designer to put on a show in Paris had been Mary Quant in the 1960s, so many critics were unsure about Vivienne's chances of success. Vivienne was unable to book the official site for Paris shows, the Coeur du Louvre. Instead, 'Buffalo' was shown at a tearoom. A chronic shortage of money limited the extravagance of the show, but 'Buffalo' impressed the media and other designers. However, few orders came in to offset the costs.

Despite her growing professional reputation, Vivienne faced a series of cash crises. Malcolm took legal action to stop a deal she had made with the Italian designer Elio Fiorucci. He believed that Vivienne's

Models in clothes from the 'Buffalo' collection, the first British collection to be shown in the French capital since the 1960s.

designs, like the stocks of their shops, were the joint property of the former partners. The dispute proved costly and Nostalgia of Mud had to close. Her personal finances, always a source of chaos, dwindled and in 1983 she was declared **bankrupt**.

Italian jobs

In 1984, Vivienne moved to D'Amario's flat in Milan. The Italians had always appreciated her designs, but legal arguments with McLaren stood in the way of any new deals. Although a leading designer, Giorgio Armani, had agreed to help produce Westwood **lines** of clothing, he began to hear rumours that Vivienne had a reputation for being difficult to work with. And when his business manager Sergio Galeotti died in 1985, Armani decided to cut all outside ties. Soon afterwards, Vivienne's relationship with D'Amario ended. It was time to go home.

With debts still outstanding, and still registered as a bankrupt, Vivienne could not trade under her own name. Her mother and her son Joseph agreed to become directors of a new company that would run Vivienne's business. The successful designer Jeff Banks also lent Vivienne money and offered her business advice. Vivienne reopened the World's End shop in July 1986.

She set about creating a new collection, which would mark her return to England. Working alone (except for a temporary assistant) and with virtually no equipment, she assembled a collection that celebrated –

and at the same time gently mocked – traditional British fashion. The 'Harris Tweed' collection, taking its name from and featuring this traditional British material, was shown at the Olympia Exhibition Centre in London. The collection was a triumph, and led to a series of valuable deals around the world.

Harris Tweed is a traditional material that has been used in British fashion for centuries. Vivienne was to bring it bang up to date.

Spreading her wings

The 'Harris Tweed' collection might have seemed a rather 'safe' way of returning to the forefront of the fashion world, but Vivienne had begun to operate as a businesswoman rather than as a rebel with little idea of profit or sales. It did, however, take real daring to use such a traditional raw material as the inspiration for what turned out to be a much-imitated range of clothing. As usual, Vivienne had done her research thoroughly. This time, the research took her back to her Derbyshire roots in search of traditional materials.

One of her suppliers was the John Smedley mill, which had been operating near Tintwistle, where Vivienne was brought up, since 1784. This was not the sort of company that anyone associated with 'cutting edge' fashions – much less those of someone who had helped launch the **Punk** scene! Vivienne travelled to the mill to discuss woollens, surprising the manager by choosing 'the colours we were about to drop because nobody had been buying them for ten years'.

Malcolm McLaren, who had advised Vivienne on most of her collections, played no part in the 'Harris Tweed' show. The tweed set the tone for what could have seemed simply a checklist of British traditional fashion, including blazers, twinsets and pearls. But Vivienne's imagination made the designs look fresh and even playful. Her choice of accompanying music, a mixture of classical, folk song and Northern brass band, also signalled her distance from Malcolm's rock and roll style.

The rhythm of success

Throughout the mid-1980s, Vivienne developed ideas that were based in traditional fashion, but given new direction thanks to her

> " *I was kind of gambling really, doing fashion shows that cost an awful lot of money was something I shouldn't have been doing.* "
> Vivienne Westwood, on 'Harris Tweed' and other shows after her return to London

imagination. No longer needing to make outrageous statements of rebellion, she could make her fashion points through subtle variations in traditional cuts or materials. Throughout this period, she was able to rely on several close friends for advice and practical help. Gary Ness, Vivienne's artist friend, helped keep her focused on matters of culture and art, which in turn helped to give Vivienne confidence about her new designs. On a practical level, fellow designer Jeff Banks guaranteed the rent for a studio Vivienne had set up in North London. By 1988, she had ten people working in this studio.

The model Sara Stockbridge wears a crown from Westwood's 'Harris Tweed' collection. The collection was a massive success.

> 'I don't accept the easy "No". I want the difficult "Yes".'
> A Vivienne Westwood phrase, which she repeats to her staff

It was in this setting, resembling a larger, busier version of Vivienne's cluttered flat, that each new collection was researched, designed, refined and prepared for showing. Having shown a flair for creating new interest in traditional British fashion **motifs**, Vivienne turned her attention to classical Greece. The 'Pagan' series of collections (1988 to 1990) featured classical Greek features such as winged sandals and flowing tunics. The collections were successes and other international designers copied the ideas.

Foreign attachments

Despite her success, Vivienne's finances were still a source of concern. Suppliers had to issue reminder notices for unpaid invoices and the staff sometimes went without pay. So it was hardly surprising that, in 1989, Vivienne accepted the offer to become Professor of Fashion at the Vienna Academy of Applied Arts. As well being proud of this recognition of her international importance as a designer, Vivienne was attracted by the money – £4000 per month for only three days' work!

She genuinely enjoyed the work in Vienna (and a similar posting later in Berlin). Her experience as a teacher came in handy as she passed on her knowledge. Some of the students, knowing of her Punk background and reputation as an **iconoclast**, might have been surprised by her techniques. Vivienne instructed them to copy historic costumes over and over again, examining each seam and stitch, the method that she used herself.

Vivienne fell in love with one of her students in Vienna, twenty-five-year-old Andreas Kronthaler. He returned to live with Vivienne in London and began to influence Vivienne's designs as well. Andreas's sense of extravagance, combined with Vivienne's eye for historical dress, led to a series of collections that some people described as **camp**. The personal and professional relationship remained strong, and they married in 1992.

Vivienne Westwood and her second husband, Andreas Kronthaler.

During this time, Vivienne's financial problems began to settle down. This improvement was in large part due to the efforts of Vivienne's old friend Carlo D'Amario, who had become business manager of Vivienne's company. This arrangement suited both of them: Vivienne was able to concentrate on the creative side of the business, and Carlo had a clear hand in steering the company in a profit-making direction.

Recognition

It was only at the end of the 1980s and the beginning of the 1990s that Vivienne began to receive the recognition that she deserved. She appeared on television, as a guest on the 'Wogan' programme and as the subject of a 'South Bank Show' documentary. In June 1990, Vivienne became the first designer to exhibit for Pitti Immagine, an exclusive Italian fashion promoter. The show, entitled 'Cut & Slash', marked another, more personal 'first': it was the first Westwood menswear collection. The title of the collection reflected the patterns of slashes that were cut or knitted into the fabrics. This distinctive feature harked back to Vivienne's own history, as she had used the technique during her Punk years.

That same year, Vivienne received another honour: the prestigious Designer of the Year Award, presented by the British Fashion Council (BFC). Many in the fashion and design world felt that this particular award was long overdue. As if to make up for previous omissions, the BFC presented her with the same award in 1991. To round off this flurry of honours came one that many would have thought unthinkable back in the wild days of the Queen's **Silver Jubilee**. In December 1992, Vivienne made the trip to Buckingham Palace to receive the OBE from the Queen. By that time Vivienne had already been nicknamed 'Queen Viv' by an affectionate public.

The Westwood logo

The Orb, Vivienne's logo, is a conscious link with two very British institutions, Harris Tweed and the British monarchy. Harris Tweeds represent the essence of British tradition in many people's eyes, yet despite its own use of a globe-like symbol for many years, the firm knows better than to criticize Vivienne's transformation. Indeed, it actually benefits greatly from its ties with one of Britain's most original creative minds. Unlike the Harris Tweed globe, the Westwood Orb is surrounded by a satellite ring. This represents the future and also acknowledges Vivienne's international outlook.

The second link, that with the monarchy, adds an extra twist, especially given Vivienne's Punk background. The Queen herself uses an orb as part of the royal **regalia** when she opens Parliament.

The Westwood orb logo.

49

Always the rebel?

By the early 1990s, Vivienne Westwood had established herself as one of the world's most influential designers. 'Established' seems an appropriate word, since she now had the acceptance and approval of the same British **Establishment** that she had once scorned. Honoured by Buckingham Palace, photographed by famous photographer Lord Snowdon, and with fashion lover Lady McAlpine wearing a Westwood outfit to the state opening of Parliament, Vivienne Westwood seemed almost a new person. Fashion critics and the general public wondered whether the playful, **provocative** edge that underscored Vivienne's designs would be blunted and made somehow 'safer'.

The answer, evident in Vivienne and the designs themselves, was no. She was absorbing traditional materials and styles to inspire her own imaginative **lines** of clothing. She had never turned her back on tradition; instead, she had always used tradition to further her own ends. Her writing on fashion has reflected this approach (see page 52). Also, the more efficient business approach of the company opened up

Vivienne poses with Princess Michael of Kent at Kensington Palace for the June 1992 'Court Couture' exhibition celebrating royal fashion past and present.

many 'mainstream' markets that were once well outside the Westwood scope. For example, a less expensive range of Westwood clothes featured in mail order catalogues for Littlewoods in the UK.

Unlikely partners

With Vivienne's reputation secure, and her clothes selling well, many avenues opened up for the Westwood lines. The Westwood flair could add a note of modernity and liveliness to other established and more conventional companies. One of the most striking examples was the **collaboration** with the London-based shop Liberty. Established in 1875, Liberty had built a reputation for providing clothes and fabrics that were brightly coloured yet tasteful. The store began stocking Westwood clothes in 1992, but in the following year it invited Vivienne to create some designs for its own goods. The collection, called 'On Liberty', was shown in March 1994, and was well received.

The deal was yet another feather in Vivienne's cap. Liberty was the sort of store whose customers would have been shocked by the Westwood designs of the 1970s and early 1980s. Liberty, for its part, had seen how the Westwood connection had breathed new life into established firms such as John Smedley's and Harris Tweeds.

In 1982, local neighbours had fiercely resisted the opening of Westwood's 'Nostalgia of Mud' shop, which was located in a highly exclusive part of London. Little did they realize that, within ten years, Vivienne would succeed in positioning herself at the very heart of the British fashion establishment.

Even more unlikely collaborations followed. In 1993, Vivienne teamed up with Brintons, one of Britain's most established carpet manufacturers, for an advertising campaign. She created a range of clothes for the campaign, made solely from carpet materials, changed only by sanding down the rough carpet backing. The advertisements were a huge success, and within weeks, people were asking Brintons

> "
> 'It is no wonder that I view with irony the nostalgia in fashion which had a uniform for everything – **regalia** for the Queen… tartan for the romantic Scots, safari suits for shooting tigers, a top hat and umbrella for the Zulu chief and a cloth cap and muffler for the docker. Uniforms for soldiers and sailors, school children, scouts, sportsmen and Indian policemen. Yet, it's all so attractive! The Barbour and the headscarf worn over the tulle ball gown and tiara…; the city gent and the endless possibilities of city stripes; the naughty school girl… with her boy's shirt and crooked tie; the lovely soft tweeds or hard ones that will keep out thorns and the rain, or worn threadbare like a Lord pretending to be poor.'
> "
>
> Vivienne Westwood, writing in 1999

for the 'Vivienne Westwood carpets'. In 1998, the Westwood company
launched a perfume, called 'Boudoir', with the German cosmetics
company Lancaster.

There were some surprises on the clothing front as well. In 1992,
Vivienne introduced bridal wear to her lines for the first time. Typically
for Britain's most notorious rebel designer, Westwood's popular made-
to-order wedding dresses have not been limited to the traditional white.
Tartan has become a Westwood favourite (see page 55) and the
Anglomania Collection of Autumn/Winter 1993/94 gave the world a
tartan wedding gown complete with exuberantly coloured net petticoats.

Vivienne's famous super-elevated shoes
are on permanent display in the Victoria
& Albert Museum, London.

Measures of success

As the millennium (and her own sixtieth birthday) approached, Vivienne Westwood and her company enjoyed a variety of new business opportunities, both in Britain and abroad. In the late 1990s, a number of Westwood stores opened outside London. The company did not own these outlets; instead they operated as **franchises**. Westwood clothes also sold well in Asia, either as one of several designer ranges in fashion stores, or under **license**. These Asian connections had some unexpected benefits; in 1996, for example, the Japanese **licensee** Itochu invested £20 million in a new Westwood store in London.

Here Vivienne is pictured dressing a dummy with one of her latest designs. Despite her international success, she continues to maintain a 'back to basics' approach and remains heavily involved in every stage of the design process.

Creating a tartan

Vivienne Westwood's standing has let her take the fast lane into the world of traditional British clothing. Tartans represent one of Scotland's (and Britain's) most traditional designs, conjuring up images of clan chiefs and pitched battles. In 1993, Vivienne created both a tartan and a clan for her Autumn/Winter collection. It normally takes two hundred years for a tartan to be recognized by Lochcarron Tweeds. However, Vivienne's 'Mac Andreas' tartan (a tribute to her husband) is already on show in the official tartan museum at Lochcarron, Scotland.

Capturing the market

By 2002 Vivienne Westwood was producing her clothes under four labels:

- The least 'formal' of the Westwood labels, Anglomania, was launched in 1997. It is geared towards younger buyers, both male and female, and is not shown on the **catwalks**.
- The ready-to-wear Red Label Collection is usually shown in London, and celebrates Vivienne's love of colour.
- The 'top of the line' Gold Label collection is produced in the United Kingdom, with regular shows in Paris. It celebrates British fashion tradition and materials while producing an effect that is sexy and elegant. Most of the garments are made to measure in the tradition of **haute couture**.
- The Westwood menswear label, MAN is largely influenced by Vivienne's husband Andreas, MAN gives traditional British tailoring a new twist, with unexpected combinations of fabrics and cuts.

Old and new

The address where it all began – 430 King's Road – remains very much part of the Westwood presence in London. The famous backward spinning clock above World's End signals that Vivienne Westwood – as both a person and 'brand-name' – can still be unsettling. Inside are Anglomania clothes and accessories and other goods aimed at the young. In keeping with its up-market address, the Vivienne Westwood shop at 6 Davies Street, Mayfair, features the haute couture Gold Label collection. Stocking the MAN collection as well as the Red Label Line, the 43 Conduit Street boutique falls somewhere in between these extremes. It is here that Vivienne Westwood can be found at her most accessible.

Timeline

1941	Vivienne Isabel Swire born in Derbyshire on 8 April
1945	Second World War ends
1954	Dora Swire (Vivienne's mother) becomes village postmistress in Tintwistle
1957	Swire family moves to Harrow, West London
1962	Vivienne Swire marries Derek Westwood
1963	Benjamin Westwood born on 3 September
1965	Vivienne Westwood meets Malcolm Edwards (later McLaren), a friend of her brother Gordon
1966	Vivienne and Derek Westwood divorce
1967	Vivienne and Malcolm move into their own flat Malcolm enrols at Croydon College of Art Vivienne returns to teaching to help make ends meet Joseph Corré (Vivienne and Malcolm's son) is born on 30 November
1968	Vivienne remains in London while Malcolm witnesses major social changes in Paris Vivienne joins Malcolm briefly in the south of France
1969–70	Vivienne takes the two boys to live in her aunt's caravan in North Wales
1970	Malcolm finds new flat in south London and is reunited with Vivienne and the two boys
1971	Let It Rock opens at 430 King's Road, London. The shop soon builds a reputation and helps to inspire a new taste for **retro** fashion.
1973	Too Fast To Live Too Young To Die (TFTLTYTD) replaces Let It Rock at 430 King's Road, London Vivienne is one of several influential young women featured in a magazine article on London life
1974	SEX replaces Too Fast To Live Too Young To Die at 430 King's Road, London
1975	The Sex Pistols are formed Using some suggestions from the band members, Vivienne creates daring outfits for the Sex Pistols

56

1976 Seditionaries replaces SEX at 430 King's Road

1977 Vivienne Westwood and Malcolm McLaren are arrested on 7 June, after Sex Pistols **Silver Jubilee** boat incident on the River Thames

1978 Following the break-up of the Sex Pistols, Malcolm moves to Paris while Vivienne remains in London
Vivienne spends long periods studying the history of fashion in the Wallace Collection museum and the fashion galleries of the Victoria & Albert Museum

1980 World's End opens at 430 King's Road, replacing Seditionaries. Its interior is designed to resemble the decking of a pirate ship.

1981 Vivienne Westwood's first collection ('Pirates') is shown in London

1982 Nostalgia of Mud opens
Vivienne Westwood's first collection to be shown in Paris ('Buffalo') is launched

1983 Final parting of Vivienne Westwood and Malcolm McLaren
Following a series of disputes with Malcolm, Vivienne is declared bankrupt
Vivienne moves to Italy, closing World's End

1986 Vivienne Westwood returns to England; World's End reopens after a two year absence
Vivienne begins to use traditional British textile companies to supply materials for her new designs

1987 'Harris Tweed' collection marks Vivienne Westwood's return to the fashion forefront

1989 Vivienne Westwood begins a two-year period as Professor of Fashion in Vienna

1990 Vivienne Westwood is honoured as Designer of the Year in the UK
A new shop ('Vivienne Westwood') opens at Davies Street, London
Vivienne unveils her first menswear collection

1991 Vivienne Westwood receives the Designer of the Year award for the second year running

1992 Awarded the OBE
Appointed honorary Senior Fellow at the Royal College of Art
Marries Andreas Kronthaler
New 'Vivienne Westwood' shop opens at Conduit Street,
in London
Liberty, the highly respected London store, begins to stock
Westwood clothes

1993 Works as Professor of Fashion at the Hochschule (Berlin)
New 'Mac Andreas' tartan is introduced as part of the
'Anglomania' collection
Vivienne teams up with Liberty to create a new collection ('On
Liberty') based on Liberty fabrics

1994 Contributes a mail-order range of clothing for the Littlewoods
catalogue (UK)

1995 Vivienne Westwood offices move to Elcho Street, Battersea
(South London)

1996 'MAN', the Westwood menswear label, is launched

1998 The first Westwood scent ('Boudoir') is introduced

1999 The first 'Vivienne Westwood' shop opens in New York

2001 Vivienne Westwood is featured in a special '**Radical** Fashion'
exhibition at the Victoria & Albert Museum, London
The Westwood 2002 Spring Collection, 'Fairy Tale', is
launched in Paris in October

Glossary

absurdist aiming to demonstrate that human beings live in a meaningless world

aesthetic study of beauty in relation to the arts

anarchist person who believes in anarchy, a political condition in which people are not ruled by a central force or government

authentic genuine, not an imitation

avant garde referring to artists and artistic movements that are at the forefront of new thinking, often leading the way in matters of taste and judgement

bankrupt legally unable to pay off all of one's debts and therefore unable to own or manage a company

biker motorcyclist, often a member of a menacing gang

bondage a style of fashion in which people pretend to tie up ('bind') and physically control each other

buyer someone from a major clothing store who attends fashion collections and agrees to buy set amounts from the designer

camp deliberately artificial or exaggerated

catwalk narrow walkway extending into a seated area, allowing people (such as fashion models) to be seen clearly by the audience

collaboration willing, and sometimes informal, partnership

conservatism preference for keeping things (such as fashion and social values) the way they always have been

controversy prolonged argument or disagreement

critical momentum point at which a process begins to continue on its own, without outside input

curator person in charge of a museum or similar collection

custom-made designed and made according to someone's requests and requirements

decorum sense of stability and calmness

drainpipe (in fashion) a style of trouser leg that is straight and narrow

Establishment general term referring to elements in society (for example, political and religious leaders, the wealthy and well-educated) whose opinions shape the way people live

franchise member of a chain of local firms that pay a fee to do business under a well-known company name

free love sexual relations without the social controls of marriage

haute couture French for 'high fashion', the most fashionable and influential designing and dressmaking

hippy young person in the 1960s who wore colourful and often loose clothes, and who favoured **free love** and individual freedom

iconoclast someone who has no respect for existing rules (about behaviour, musical taste and so on)

impresario person who puts on commercial entertainment of various kinds

inflammatory deliberately trying to stir up feelings or to cause offence

license fee paid to sell a certain type of product (such as clothing from a particular company)

licensee person or company that obtains a commercial license

line (in fashion) overall selection of clothing from a particular company

logo easily recognizable image that identifies a company

mentor someone who acts as a friendly adviser or teacher

minimalist (in artistic terms) having as little extra decoration as possible

Mods British youth 'tribe' whose members shared a taste for well-tailored 'cool' outfits

motifs distinctive and recurring shapes

pageantry highly organized rituals and ceremonies

pornographic using sexual images

propaganda (sometimes misleading or false) information that aims to influence people's thinking on certain issues

provocative prompting an extreme reaction in others

Punk young people in the 1970s who adopted a style of clothing and behaviour that was meant to shock the public

radical favouring extreme change

rationing (in Britain after the Second World War) setting a limit to the sale of certain foods and other goods

regalia collected emblems of royalty

retro a style of clothing imitating fashion from the recent past

revolution total overthrow of an existing system of government or thinking

sedition stirring up discontent or rebellion against a government

Silver Jubilee twenty-fifth anniversary of something

slogan memorable catchphrase linked with a group

street credibility ability to wear the latest popular fashions confidently and without feeling self-conscious

superfluous unnecessary

synonymous always associated with

Teddy Boys group of British rock and roll lovers from the 1950s, who wore long jackets and tight trousers (men) and wide hooped skirts and dresses (women)

tyranny harsh and undemocratic rule

Websites, places of interest and further reading

Websites

http://www.viviennewestwood.com
Here you can find information on the Gold Label, Man, Anglomania and Red Label collections. The site allows you to view the latest collections alongside Westwood's shops, accessories and perfume.

http://www.fashion-icon.com/blur/
This website gives an upbeat portrayal of Vivienne Westwood, placing her among the most influential designers at work today.

http://www.astronart.co.uk/vivdes.htm
This site acts as an introduction to Vivienne Westwood and her work. It is especially helpful in showing how traditional British textiles have inspired a range of Westwood collections.

Further reading

Fashion and Perversity: A Life of Vivienne Westwood and the Sixties Laid Bare, Fred Vermorel (Bloomsbury, 1996)

Vivienne Westwood, Catherine McDermott (Fantail, 1999)

Vivienne Westwood, Catherine McDermott and Edwina Ehrman (Philip Wilson Publishers, 2000)

Vivienne Westwood: A London Fashion, Vivienne Westwood, et al (Philip Wilson Publishers, 2000)

Vivienne Westwood: An Unfashionable Life, Jane Mulvagh (HarperCollins, 1998)

Vivienne Westwood (Universe of Fashion), Gene Krell and Maud Molyneux (Thames and Hudson, 1997)

The Wicked Ways of Malcolm McLaren, Craig Bromberg (Omnibus Press, 1991)

Show rooms

France

Vivienne Westwood France
13 rue du Mail
75002 Paris
Tel: (33) 01 4927 0023

Italy

Vivienne Westwood Milan
Via Cerva 17/19
20122 Milan
Tel: (39) 02 7602 3429

Japan

Vivienne Westwood Japan
Iriki Building 3F
3-5-3-Kita Aoyama
Minato-ku
107-0061 Tokyo
Tel: (81) 03 3401 9507

UK

World's End
430 King's Road
London
SW10 0LJ
Tel: (44) 207 7352 6551

USA

Vivienne Westwood New York
71 Greene Street
New York
NY 10012
Tel: (1) 212 334 1500

Index